Happy language learning!

♡ Ann
A Rambling Hafie

The True Story of an Orange Tabby Cat and a Multicultural Family

一只虎斑橘猫和一个多元文化家庭之间的真实故事

Narrated from a Cat's Perspective
以一只猫的视角讲述

©2023 A Halfie's Rambles LLC
Fort Worth, Texas
德克萨斯州沃斯堡
Email: halfiesrambles@outlook.com
http://www.halfiesrambles.com

Den Chan — The Cat Who Crossed the Ocean —
3 Bilingual Children's Book Versions: Japanese & English, English & Chinese, Chinese & Japanese

Den酱 — 漂洋过海的猫 —
3册双语儿童绘本: 日英对照, 英中对照, 中日对照

Proudly printed and bound in the State of Texas, U.S.A.
本书于美国德克萨斯州印刷和装订。

ISBN 979-8-9891824-1-1
Library of Congress Control Number: 2023919832

Published by A Halfie's Rambles LLC
All rights reserved. No part of this book may be used or reproduced in any form whatsoever without permission except in the case of brief quotations in articles or reviews.

由A Halfie's Rambles LLC出版
若无版权持有人的书面授权，任何人不得复制、仿造、再版、下载、公布、扩散或传播任何文本、图像、图形、标识、按钮、图标、图片等内容，用作任何商业及公共用途。

I would like to express my heartfelt gratitude to my wonderful siblings, Akira, Aya, and Tessa Katagiri; and my father, Dr. Yasuhiro Katagiri. Thank you for your unwavering love and encouragement throughout the production process of this book.

To my dear friends, Jocelyn Li, Patricia & Scott Bailey, Melanie Page, Erin Fukayama, Haley Johnson, and Jade Li; thank you for the unique insights with which you supported this endeavor of mine.

I relied greatly on each and every one of your linguistic acumen and diverse perspectives to bring this book to life. Thank y'all so much.

特别感谢我优秀的兄弟姐妹,Akira, Aya和Tessa Katagiri, 以及我的父亲Yasuhiro Katagiri, 感谢你们在本书创作过程中给予的关爱和鼓励。

我亲爱的朋友们,李盛霖、Patricia & Scott Bailey、梅勒妮 帕赫、Erin Fukayama、Haley Johnson 和李园,感谢你们以独特的见解支持我。

此书的问世,离不开你们每个人的语言专长和不同视角的加持。非常感谢你们。

Dear Readers,

This book is based on a true story, following the adventures of Den Chan, an orange tabby cat who moved from Japan to America.
The three children in this book also share the same story.

Our world is vast, and I want children to see and explore such a world. If you have ever shared this thought, this is a perfect book to pick up and read with your children.

Written in hope to inspire the next generation to have the interest and courage to explore our vast world,

A Rambling Halfie,
Ann R. Katagiri

亲爱的读者们，

本书由真实故事改编，讲述了一只从日本搬到美国的虎斑橘猫Den酱的生活。本书提到的三个孩子也有着同样的经历。

我们的世界如此广阔，我希望孩子们能看到并愿意探索这样的世界。如果你也有同样的想法，这是一本你应该跟自己的孩子们一起阅读的书。

带着激励下一代的兴趣和勇气去探索广阔世界的希望而写，

漫谈的混血儿，
片桐 晏

Dedicated to Den Chan,
who was a loving cat to all.
献给Den酱，一只对所有人都
充满爱心的猫。

Den Chan

The Cat Who Crossed the Ocean

Written by Ann R. Katagiri   Illustrated by Yuriko Hamada

Den酱
漂洋过海的猫

文 片桐 晏　绘 浜田 由美子

A Halfie's Rambles LLC

My name is Den. I was born in Japan.

Everyone calls me Den Chan.

wǒ de míng zì jiào　　　wǒ zài rì běn chū shēng
我的名字叫Den，我在日本出生。
dà jiā dōu jiào wǒ　jiàng
大家都叫我Den酱。

This name was given to me because of my golDEN fur.

wǒ shì jīn sè　　　　　de
我是金色(golDEN)的，
zhè jiù shì wǒ míng zì de yóu lái
这就是我名字的由来。

bobtail
duǎn duǎn de wěi ba
短短的尾巴

Since birth, I had been a stray cat.

自出生以来，我就在流浪。

I was making the most of life with my mother and siblings.

我和我的兄弟姐妹，还有妈妈一起努力的生活。

One day, I saw some children playing outside.
yǒu yì tiān wǒ kàn dào le zài wài mian wán shuǎ de hái zi men
有一天，我看到了在外面玩耍的孩子们。

Those children were playing catch with a tennis ball, so I became curious.
tā men zài wán jiē wǎng qiú
他们在玩接网球，
zhè ràng wǒ fēi cháng hào qí
这让我非常好奇。

I could not help myself from wanting to play with the flying tennis ball.

我止不住地想玩那个飞来飞去的网球。

My siblings were frightened, but I gathered all my courage to jump out from the bushes I was hiding behind.

我的兄弟姐妹们都很害怕，但我鼓起了所有的勇气，从藏身的灌木丛中跳了出来。

The three children were very kind and showed interest in me.

这三个孩子们都非常友善，对我表现出了浓厚的兴趣。

As we played with each other, they started feeding me delicious snacks.

我们一起玩耍，他们还喂我吃好吃的。

Since the children were so kind and the yummy treats were so good,
I began to visit their home every day.

wǒ bèi hái zi men de shàn liáng hé měi wèi jiā yáo suǒ xī yǐn
我被孩子们的善良和美味佳肴所吸引，
wǒ biàn měi tiān dōu qù bài fǎng tā men de jiā
我便每天都去拜访他们的家。

They even made a cozy bed just for me using some towels and a cardboard box, always loving on me.

他们甚至用纸箱铺上毛巾
为我做了个舒适的小窝,
并给了我很多的爱。

Trying my best to show my thanks,

I gave them bugs and small birds caught nearby,

as well as fried shrimp I found in the garbage.

为了尽我最大努力表示感谢，我捉来了虫子、小鸟，
还在垃圾中找到了炸虾送给他们。

They always said, "Thank you, Den Chan."

他们总是对我说："谢谢你，Den 酱。"

A year passed and the children and their family decided to move to America, so I became very sad.

_{yì nián guò qù le   zhè yì jiā rén jué dìng}
一年过去了, 这一家人决定
_{bān dào měi guó shēng huó   wǒ gǎn dào fēi cháng nán guò}
搬到美国生活, 我感到非常难过。

I thought we would never see each other again.

_{wǒ hěn pà huì zài yě jiàn bú dào tā men le}
我很怕会再也见不到他们了。

So, on the day they told me
they wanted to take me with them,
joy filled my heart.

^{yīn cǐ dāng tā men gào sù wǒ xiǎng dài wǒ yì qǐ qù de}
因此，当他们告诉我想带我一起去的
^{nà yì tiān wǒ gāo xìng jí le}
那一天，我高兴极了。

It was the happiest day of
my stray-cat life.

^{nà shì wǒ liú làng shēng huó zhōng}
那是我流浪生活中
^{zuì kuài lè de yì tiān}
最快乐的一天。

My biggest struggle was wondering if a cat like me, who grew up and spent his whole life in Japan, could survive in another country.

我最担心的是，像我这样一辈子都生活在日本的猫能否在国外生存呢？

As a Japanese cat, would people say I look weird?

我是一只日本猫，别人会说我看起来很奇怪吗？

Even then, looking forward to the upcoming adventure, my heart was beating with excitement.

但我很期待即将到来的冒险，我的心激动地跳动着。

I had always wondered what other countries there were in the world.

我一直都想知道世界上还有哪些国家。

To prepare to travel to America, I went to the animal hospital and got a *microchip put in my neck.

wèi le zhǔn bèi chū guó wǒ qù le dòng wù yī yuàn
为了准备出国，我去了动物医院，
bìng zài bó zi shàng qiàn rù le yí kuài wēi xīn piàn
并在脖子上嵌入了一块微芯片*。

The doctor said it was for my safety.

yī shēng shuō zhè shì wèi le wǒ de ān quán
医生说这是为了我的安全。

*A microchip is a small, electronic device about the size of a grain of rice. Placed under the skin of an animal, it is used as a way to identify pets and prove their immunization.

*微芯片是一种嵌入于动物皮下的小型电子设备，米粒大小，作为识别宠物和证明其免疫的一种方法。

My first ride on an airplane seemed long and scary.

But as the airplane took off, I knew everything would be okay since I was with a family who loved me.

由于这是我第一次乘坐飞机,看起来是又漫长又恐怖的。

但当飞机起飞时,我就知道自己会没事的,因为我和爱我的家人们在一起。

After crossing the ocean, the airplane arrived.

Then my family came to pick me up.

yuè guò hǎi yáng　　fēi jī dào dá hòu　　wǒ de jiā rén lái jiē wǒ
越过海洋，飞机到达后，我的家人来接我。

Having arrived in a strange country,

I kept meowing out of fear.

They held me softly and pet my head.

gāng dào yí gè mò shēng de guó jiā　　wǒ yì zhí hài pà de miāo miāo jiào
刚到一个陌生的国家，我一直害怕地喵喵叫。
tā men qīng qīng de bào zhe wǒ　　fǔ mō wǒ de tóu
他们轻轻地抱着我，抚摸我的头。

After arriving at our new home,
my body did not move like normal due to jet lag,
and I had to get used to American cat food.

到了新家之后，时差反应再加上不得不适应美国的猫粮，
我的身体无法正常行动。

But as time passed, I began to get used to
life in America and started to love it.

但随着时间的流逝，我慢慢地适应，
并越来越喜欢美国的生活。

Unlike Japan, in America, people speak English.

However, since my family had spoken with me in both English and Japanese, it was not too hard for me to adapt.

与日本不同，在美国，人们讲英语。

但是因为我的家人从一开始就用英语和日语和我说话，所以适应起来并不难。

Other than language, I am sure there will be more hard things in the future.
除了语言，将来肯定还会有更加艰难的事情。

But thinking back on that first day I played with the children in Japan, I feel like I can stand up to anything.
但我一想起和孩子们在日本一起玩儿的那一天，我认为我可以面对任何情况。

You see, by having enough courage, I found a family...
a family that loves me like one of their own.

你看，我用了足够的勇气，结果，我找到了一个家……
有着像爱自己孩子们一样爱我的家人们。

Like me, Den Chan, what courageous thing would you like to do?

像Den酱我这样，
你想做些什么勇敢的事情呢?

Den Chan's Journey
Den酱的旅途
jiàng de lǚ tú

America
měi guó
美国

TEXAS
dé kè sà sī zhōu
德克萨斯州

JAPAN
rì běn
日本

Ann R. Katagiri is a self-proclaimed "Rambling Halfie" who loves to share blog posts with others using her native languages (English & Japanese) as well as Mandarin Chinese, which she began learning during college.

A child to a blonde-haired, blue-eyed Texan mother and a Japanese father who is a historian of the American South, Ann was born in Mississippi while her father was a Fulbright scholar from Japan. Her childhood was spent in Japan until she moved to Texas when she was 14 years old. She grew up speaking English and Japanese, learning Chinese later in life after falling in love with China's food, culture, and language when studying abroad. She was beyond happy to call Beijing her home for over three years. All of her inspiration is credited to having lived in the three different countries of the languages she speaks. This is her debut children's book.

Since 2019, her endeavor to provide advertisement-free, honest blog posts continues as a monthly trilingual blog post in English, Japanese, and Chinese. You can find her rambles in these three languages at www.halfiesrambles.com.

片桐晏自称是"写漫谈的混血儿"。她热衷于用她的母语（英语和日语）和在上大学时开始学习的中文（普通话）与他人分享各种各样的话题。她积极写作，为大家提供无广告、真实的博客文章。
晏在金发碧眼的德克萨斯母亲和身为美国南部历史博士的日本父亲家庭长大。当她父亲作为一名富布赖特学者的时候，她在密西西比州出生。她的童年是在日本度过的，14岁时搬到德克萨斯州。从小就讲英语和日语，在中国留学后，爱上了中国的食物、文化和语言，便开始学习中文。她非常欣喜于在北京安家三年多的经历。她所有的灵感都归功于她在所讲语言的三个国家生活过的经历。这是她的首部儿童书。
自2019年起，她努力提供真实，无广告的博文，持续以每月用英语，日语和中文博文的形式发布。你可以在 www.halfiesrambles.com 找到她用三种语言所写的漫谈。

Illustrated by Melanie Page
绘：梅勒妮 帕赫

@DenChanTheCatBook

/AHalfiesRambles

halfiesrambles.com

Yuriko Hamada is an illustrator based in Fukuoka, Japan who specializes in a wide range of literary fields such as advertisements, publications, packages, and videos. This is her debut children's book illustration.

Within the digital field, she utilizes 3DCG and paint software when creating her works. She is also well versed in analog (traditional) forms of producing illustration works, incorporating materials such as Japanese-style paints and watercolors. She takes great care to authentically convey feelings of awe and beauty through her illustrations and works (both still and moving images), all the while challenging herself in a wide range of fields.

She is particularly attracted to the essential beauty of natural scenes, living creatures, and traditional arts and culture that should be passed on to future generations. Cherishing the spirit of "wa" ("unity"), which is deeply rooted in Japanese culture, she hopes to exhibit its concepts and values in her own works.

In her free time, she loves spending time at bookstores, surfing the internet to gather information at her leisure, enjoying delicious tea and sweets, watching movies, and listening to music.

浜田由美子是日本福冈的一名插画家，擅长广告、出版物、包装和视频等广泛的文学领域。这是她首次为儿童图书绘制插图。
在数字领域，她使用 3DCG 和绘画软件创作作品。她还精通以模拟（传统）形式制作插图作品，结合使用日式颜料和水彩等材料。她非常注重通过插图和作品（包括静态和动态图像）真实地传达敬畏和美的感受，同时在广泛的领域挑战自己。她尤其钟情于自然景色、生物和传统艺术与文化的本质之美，并将其延续到未来。她喜欢日本文化中根深蒂固的"和"（"统一"）的精神，希望能在自己的作品中展现这种价值观。
闲暇时，她喜欢逛书店、上网收集信息、品尝美味的茶和甜点、看电影和听音乐。

@yuriko.h3

yuriko-h.com

Den Chan

The main character and inspiration behind this story, a Japanese cat, Den, was adopted as a kitten into the Katagiri family. He then moved with them across the ocean to America and was loved by his family for over 13 years.

This story is told from his perspective as a cat, but embodies the stories of the children who lovingly raised him.

When eating, he would meow as if he was saying "thank you", relished being held, and loved playing around the house. His favorite things to do were to sunbathe in the warm sun and go on walks outside.

Den酱

这个故事背后的灵感和主人公,是来自于一只日本猫Den。它在幼猫时期被片桐家收养。后来随着家人漂洋过海来到美国,被疼爱了13年之久。

整篇故事是从一只猫的角度讲述的,同时也体现了充满爱心养它的片桐家孩子们的故事。

它吃饭的时候会喵喵叫,好像在说"谢谢"一样;被人抱着的时候很开心;喜欢在家里玩耍。它最喜欢做的事情是在温暖的阳光下晒太阳和到外面散步。

Photo Credit: Aya Katagiri   照片:片桐 彩

Thank you for reading my story!

See you next time!

gǎn xiè dà jiā yuè dú wǒ de gù shi
感谢大家阅读我的故事！

wǒ men xià cì jiàn
我们下次见！